Robert Couturier

Robert Couturier

DESIGNING PARADISES

ROBERT COUTURIER
WRITTEN WITH
TIM McKEOUGH

TIM STREET-PORTER
PRINCIPAL PHOTOGRAPHER

PREFACE BY CAROLYNE ROEHM
POSTFACE BY CAROLINE WEBER

RIZZOLI
NEW YORK

New York · Paris · London · Milan

I dedicate this book to my grandparents first and foremost—I owe the best part of myself to them; to Jeffrey, to whom I owe my happiness—without him Kent would never be the earthly paradise that it is; and, of course, to my beloved pets, Henriette, Bess, Hercule, and Dora, who are the only sort of angels I trust.

— Robert Couturier

TABLE OF CONTENTS

PREFACE BY
CAROLYNE ROEHM
9

INTRODUCTION
11

PART I
PARADISE
18

THE CITY APARTMENT
102

PART II
SELECT PROJECTS
118

MEXICO
120

CITY CLASSIC
144

CITY MODERN
156

ENGLISH COUNTRYSIDE
186

POSTFACE BY
CAROLINE WEBER
221

ACKNOWLEDGMENTS
223

PREFACE

FROM THE MOMENT I FIRST MET Robert I loved him. How could anyone not? His delightful laugh, his twinkling eyes, his elegance, his intellectual inquisitiveness, and his open heart are readily evident. For me, it was his encyclopedic knowledge of two of my favorite subjects—the decorative arts and architecture of eighteenth-century France—that initially grabbed my attention.

Robert's incredible memory for the details of the beauty created during that era and the intrigues of the most powerful and influential court in the world at that time are amazing. His stories of the lives of the courtiers who inhabited the enchanting châteaus, pavilions, follies, and grand salons are mesmerizing. And then, when I discovered that Robert's love for dogs and beautiful gardens is as crazy as mine, our friendship was sealed forever.

The sensation I feel when visiting Robert and Jeffrey's country home is always the same. Not only is it delightful, but it also just feels so right. The abundant natural light and generous proportions of the rooms serve as a lovely backdrop to the cozy and elegant decoration. It showcases Robert's skill both as an architect and a decorator. Not unlike Robert Adam, one of my eighteenth-century heroes, Robert is masterful at orchestrating a symbiotic relationship between the structure, space, and decor. He gives each room a harmony not often found today. In his drawing room, there is a lovely eighteenth-century daybed positioned in front of a large window with a glorious view of the lake, where I could be happily ensconced for days. This arrangement is a wonderful focal point for the room, but it also exudes a refined sense of comfort, tranquility, and luxury. After dinners at Robert's house, I have loved sitting there with friends and, of course, the dogs, drinking coffee, laughing, and not wanting to leave.

The versatility of Robert's talent is on display from the United States to Mexico to Europe. This book highlights but a few of his projects—from the classic look of his county home in Connecticut and a historic house in England to contemporary apartments in Manhattan. La Loma, the house Robert created for Sir James Goldsmith in Mexico, is dazzling in its size as well as its beauty. Robert melds the art and elements of different periods, making the twenty-first century harmonious with earlier eras at the same time that he incorporates the personalities of his clients in their new homes. Nowhere is this more evident than in his own house. He and Jeffrey have married their very different aesthetics into a delightful, deeply personal home.

I know you will enjoy this lovely book filled with beautiful spaces, and learning about this man of such great refinement. Cecile Beaton once wrote in *The Glass of Fashion*: "When we talk about fashion, we really mean the whole art of living." Merely substitute "interior design" for "fashion"—and how aptly this describes Robert's work and life.

— Carolyne Roehm

Louis XVI furniture in a Brooklyn house designed to resemble a perfectly French eighteenth-century residence.

INTRODUCTION

I'LL NEVER FORGET MY EARLY DAYS IN
New York. I had just arrived in Manhattan from France, where I had
grown up in a world disconnected from reality. Shortly after landing my
first job at a design firm, I was tasked with completing a construction
inspection for a new private residence. I took the assignment to heart,
arrived at the apartment attired in a way that I later discovered was over-
dressed, and set about scrutinizing every last detail, right down to the
heads of screws, searching for even the slightest imperfections. By the time
I finished, I had a long list of required fixes. The general contractor looked
at me and asked, "What, you don't like it?" I expressed that it wasn't up to
my standards. It took him just seconds to shoot me down with a few choice
expletives—and then he turned and walked off the job, leaving me in the
construction dust to figure out how we would ever complete the home.

That encounter taught me an important lesson. Although I'm still just as much of a perfectionist,
I've learned not to take myself so seriously. From my point of view, my job is to help people dream, to
make those dreams reality, and to transform abstract ideas into concrete creations. A client's emotions
about their surroundings have to be translated into forms, volumes, and colors that will generate the
background of their life. It is very indiscreet work, revealing to the outside how a person feels about
his or her private world. A successful home can only be achieved through confidence, playfulness, and
humor, even if the process is sometimes fraught with difficult moments. If the result is obtained
through conflict and argument, the spaces created will never be happy ones. Rooms are vividly tinted
by the emotions that helped spawn them. Even a pink room created in sadness will be a sad room.

I have long been a voracious reader and collector with an insatiable appetite for the decorative
arts, and I believe that my enthusiasm for the topic rubs off on the people I work with. I like seventeenth-century silver and twentieth-century silver, I like Chinese rugs and Tibetan rugs, I like Persian
and French. I like everything that has a form of aesthetic beauty, from a particularly exquisite
example of a Louis XIV armchair to the pure sculptural appeal of a curvaceous contemporary table by
Ron Arad. As a result, I also enjoy designing many different kinds of homes, from eighteenth-century
French palaces to polished ultramodern spaces to eclectic interiors that freely mix disparate elements.

Couturier's library in Kent is a quiet place for contemplation. Collected objects, including a
sixteenth-century globe depicting an incomplete world, sit atop a 1950s desk, with matching red silk velvet chair,
by Emilio Terry. The window frames a breathtaking view of the garden outside.

I often aim to make rooms feel warm and reassuring—a trait that became especially important to me after a difficult childhood. I was fortunate to have grown up in a family with financial means, but I experienced an often "untethered" upbringing. My father was not around, and when he was, I was terrified; my mother was emotionally unavailable. It's difficult to talk about one's upbringing and education because if it was bad, people may say that you're a social climber, and if good, they assume you didn't really earn your success. But in the end, it really doesn't matter. What is important are the reasons we choose one path over another.

In every room of my childhood homes, I had favorite hiding places where I soaked up the atmosphere. These rooms were filled with antique furniture, heavy damask curtains tied back with big silk tassels, and half-closed shutters that filtered light, allowing dust specks to dance on narrow sunbeams. I developed personal relationships with three-drawer *commodes tombeaux*, graceful Louis XV *fauteuils en cabriolet*, and tall, deep *fauteuils à oreillettes*. These spaces were a source of my own narratives. I could retrace the provenance of each piece from its creation to its current state. They were reassuring and never reproachful like my terrifying father.

My maternal grandmother saw trouble brewing and intervened, bringing me to live with her in her Parisian home when I was just a youngster. Antiques, furniture, and art were everywhere—Jean-Michel Frank had designed her house, and Jacques Adnet had designed the furniture in my grandfather's office. At the same time, I countered my solitude by devouring reams of French literature. My friends were the characters in the novels, and the rooms described in the books supported my decorative imagination. These artificial worlds were perfect, of course, and to this day I recall *À rebours* when thinking about heavily decorated rooms, and *Le Côté de Guermantes* when considering elegant drawing rooms. Classical music provided emotional support and reflected the moods I wanted to create—joy with

Bach and Mozart, romance with Schubert and Beethoven, power and darkness with Wagner, and wild energy with Stravinsky. And always, for peace of mind, Bach's cantatas.

When it came time to choose a profession, my philosophy teacher, who was my mentor, asked me what I enjoyed doing most. I told him that I spent hours listening to classical music and drawing "perfect" houses filled with "perfect" furniture (at least to my eyes). These rooms would be occupied by the "perfect" family: attentive parents, caring domestics, and innumerable pets. When I showed him my drawings, he said that interior design and architecture were clearly my true calling. I'm not sure I believed him at the time, since what I was doing was so highly personal. It's easy to draw a house, but more difficult to make sure it can stand up, and I needed to learn the principles of construction.

After some early missteps, I eventually enrolled at the École Camondo. My grandmother was slightly horrified at my decision. To her, you weren't supposed to be somebody who was going to work for somebody else. She said, "You're going to go into our friends' houses through the service doors." But I told her, "No, the world has changed."

I pushed ahead and spent five years studying classic and contemporary residential architecture and interior design. A busy social schedule combined with my relative disinterest in the more technical subjects, such as construction and cabinetry, led me to have a lackluster attendance record. My grades suffered as a result, but I always managed to pass and move on to the next year thanks to a natural talent for drawing that allowed me to produce perspective sketches and renderings with ease.

New York City always fascinated me. It seemed like it was a liberated place where you could be whatever you wanted, and talent was all that mattered. It was also the location of Studio 54, which for a straitlaced French boy

An armoire filled with earthenware that Couturier and Jeffrey Morgan have amassed over the years.

held all the promises of an earthly paradise. I finally arrived in the city in 1978, where I found work in the offices of Adam Tihany, an interior designer specializing in restaurants and nightclubs. Although it was an odd match for me in terms of aesthetics, I was still in the process of finding my voice as a designer. My intention was to visit Manhattan for only one summer, but I found it impossible to leave, and my move became permanent.

Adam proved to be a wonderful, generous mentor, and I quickly rose to more senior positions in his office. The timing couldn't have been better. My grandfather died in 1981, and an examination of our family's finances revealed an alarming reality—most of the money had evaporated. I realized that, from that point forward, I would have to count on my own earnings for support. It was therefore a moment of incredible good fortune when I met billionaire financier Sir James "Jimmy" Goldsmith through a chance encounter at a dinner party the very next year. Jimmy had just purchased a townhouse on Manhattan's Upper East Side and—unbelievably—asked me to look at it. I knew this was a great chance that I had been given. I think life is like that—you arrive at these crossroads and whatever you choose, it's going to change your life in many ways. I walked through the house, which hadn't been touched since 1924, offered a fresh new vision for what it could become, and was promptly hired. That commission soon led to more projects, which allowed me to establish my own firm in 1987. My relationship with Jimmy, who became something of a father figure for me, eventually led to the commission to design Cuixmala—his extravagant twenty-thousand-acre Mexican estate, which involved numerous palatial seaside residences and a village of supporting buildings, constructed by a dedicated team of one thousand workers.

But no matter how big the project, I always aim to bring a sense of levity to the design process. I value lasting friendships and crackling conversations far above any ostentatious displays of wealth. And I believe that homes should reflect the way a homeowner wants to live every day, not serve as a showcase to impress guests. I don't understand the view that what you do in your house is for others, not for you. To craft a complete environment, I always consider how a home stimulates the five senses—the feel of upholstery under the hand, the visual presentation of artifacts that draws a person through the space, the gentle echo of a grand room or the insulated envelope of an intimate space, the taste of herbs from the garden, and the subtle hints of perfume and smoldering ash that bear witness to the close of a day's activities. It's a sort of holistic way of looking at interiors—you don't favor one thing over another. It's how I wanted to design my own house too—the gardens and grounds are part of what the house is. You know precisely where you are, geographically and historically.

My husband, Jeffrey Morgan, is the person who originally attracted me to the area of Kent, Connecticut, in 1997, where we now live with our four beloved shih tzus. Jeffrey is a New England gentleman who is well versed in American decorative arts and a lover of old furnishings left untouched by the centuries, in their original state of simple perfection. He had already restored a 1742 home on the site that would eventually become our larger country retreat. At first, I struggled to understand his passion for the spartan, sometimes severe minimalism that prevailed in eighteenth-century America. (I actually teased him mercilessly, and proposed that we put sofas and armchairs inside.) But I eventually learned to see the restrained beauty of such spaces, even as I created infinitely more comfortable rooms in the new buildings we added to the property.

In the end, I have to admit that I'm completely addicted to luxury. I have no ability for anything else.

PART

I

PARADISE

AS MY RELATIONSHIP WITH JEFFREY Morgan deepened, I began to spend more time in Kent, Connecticut, where he lived in a 1742 house that felt as if one had stepped back in time. He loves nothing more than an extremely sober room full of early eighteenth-century furniture and artifacts. It became evident that I was never going to reform Jeffrey from such an old-fashioned lifestyle. He gave little attention to modern conveniences such as efficient central heating, insulated windows, and hot running water, but I could not see myself adapting to icy drafts, tepid showers, or straight-backed chairs. So we agreed to build a one-room guesthouse next door, based on an eighteenth-century schoolhouse a few miles away. Soon, the land across the street from his house became available and we bought it. Suddenly, all the hours spent daydreaming about a paradise, recalling the rooms of my childhood, bore fruit.

Although our country retreat in Kent is very simple, the grounds, which were full of huge hemlocks and old oaks, took shape in fits and starts as we found bursts of inspiration. The sixteen-acre property encompasses a series of gardens and buildings that were developed organically over time, and that continue to evolve. I designed the core of the classically proportioned main house almost on a whim one sunny afternoon in 2000. Taking a break during a hike across the hillside, I sketched what would become the basis of the house—two pavilions with a square entry hall in the middle. Rather than reworking the scheme for months on end, or delving into a range of possibilities, I moved swiftly to construction. It was very instinctive. I wasn't reflecting on how I wanted the living room or kitchen to feel. I just drew it and built it. Two years later, my sketch became reality.

Today, a winding promenade takes you past the original American house, which was Jeffrey's longtime home, before whisking you along a treelined driveway to the reconstructed Dover House, which dates from the early eighteenth-century. After ascending a gentle rise, the drive opens up and descends toward the back of the house, offering expansive views over the parterre garden, the cedar-shingle rooftops and brick chimneys, and the lapping blue waters of North Spectacle Lake beyond. There's something special about a house built on a bank compared to a home that's on top of a hill. It creates an element of surprise, and what you see from one side isn't the same as the other.

At this house, the surprises keep coming, year after year. Indeed, it will never really be completely finished. I continue to fine-tune and tinker, changing some aspects of the main house, adding new pavilions and functions, and overhauling the gardens. The result is a personal, layered property that reveals itself in stages. It keeps even frequent visitors guessing at what they might see next.

It's an odd thing to design a house for yourself. You design it at one point in time, and it gets built years later. But when you move in, you're a different person because you've had different experiences and seen other things. All of a sudden, it no longer reflects who you've become, unless you can continue to adjust it.

As a salve for that constant change, and to reflect our shifting tastes and desires, I wanted this house to be something that would evolve with us. Because it is so flexible, and allows me to pursue my ideas for country living while also collecting furniture, fabrics, art, and objects, it has gradually developed into my distinct vision of an idyllic rural home, where our dogs live pampered and carefree lives. This refuge has become the place where I am profoundly happy, where everything that is dear to me is present. I don't want to be anywhere else.

PRECEDING SPREAD: A 1760s terra-cotta sphinx in the image of Madame du Barry, mistress of Louis XV, is given pride of place on a 1720s commode by Doaras.

OPPOSITE: A pair of pinecone finials flanks a path of limestone steps.

PRECEDING SPREAD: The gardens are designed as a series of
formal parterres on terraces rising up behind the house, which provide
geometric appeal in all four seasons. The kitchen and dining room are
located in the wing of the house at the right; the living room is on the left.

OPPOSITE AND ABOVE: Couturier's initial sketch for a home
consisting of two square volumes linked by an entrance hall has expanded to
include a light-filled dining room and a stand-alone pavilion for the library.

ARRIVAL

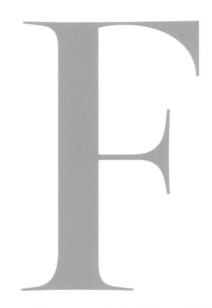

FOR SUCH A GRAND HOUSE, THE ENTRANCE to Couturier's home is surprisingly friendly in scale. Only a single story tall, it embraces visitors with a welcoming hug before releasing them into the building's larger rooms. "With architecture, one thing I've always loved is going from room to room through small and narrow corridors," says Couturier. "There's a sense of passage and surprise that's thrilling. That's how I conceived of this entrance."

But throwing open the front doors reveals another shift in scale—an enormous mirror in a patinated copper frame, which was originally part of an elaborate ceiling in a New York building, dominates the room. Even though you've just stepped inside, it immediately reflects the swaying trees and lake behind you. "That's one of the first pieces we bought for the house," says Couturier. "When you come inside, there's something special about looking back outside. It makes the wall disappear.

"There's one element from my childhood homes that I tried to re-create here—the smell of dust, humid ashes, and old-fashioned perfume," he continues. "My friend Frédéric Malle produced the scent, called Café Society, which to me offers a reminder of paradise."

At the main entrance, a pair of eighteenth-century English limestone urns creates a strong sense of symmetry. Two of Couturier's beloved dogs, Dora (in front) and Hercule, are always ready to welcome him home.

ABOVE: When the doors are thrown open, an enormous
mirror inside the entrance hall reflects idyllic views of the trees and lake.

OPPOSITE: Couturier discovered the verdigris mirror, which had been salvaged from a
building in New York, at R. T. Facts in Kent. A Louis XV *table à écrire* and armchairs
by Georges Jacob are positioned before the mirror; a hanging lantern and smaller mirrors by Serge Roche
and a seventh-century Cambodian sculpture of Harihara are seen in the reflection.

T

THE LIBRARY

THE WHOLE OF COUTURIER'S COUNTRY estate is designed as a calming escape from the frenetic energy of New York City, but when the designer truly needs a moment of quiet contemplation, he heads for the library. Set apart from the main house by only a few footsteps, it feels like a majestic hideaway in the forest. "There's no television, no telephone, nothing like that," says Couturier. "You can be there and do what you want, and nothing will interfere with your life."

When Couturier and Morgan first built the house in 2002, their original landscape designer convinced them to use an area in front of the property as an outdoor dining terrace. But a few years later, realizing that they never ate outside "largely due to annoying insects, collections of dead leaves, and outdoor furniture that quickly took on a nasty appearance," says Couturier, they decided they would be better served by an enclosed structure with a different focus. After discovering an early American Federal-style doorway and salvaged neoclassical columns at the store R. T. Facts in Kent, he set about designing a new library around the reclaimed architectural components in 2008.

Square on the outside, the building holds a handsome octagonal room within, where the floor is finished with the same black and white stone and slate used for the main house's entrance and dining room. It presents not only a portion of Couturier's extensive book collection—from tomes on art and architecture to classic volumes of American, English, French, and Russian literature displayed on four bookcases framed by Doric columns that have been split in half—but also selections of curios the designer has amassed over the years. Floor-to-ceiling windows offer masterfully framed views of the natural world—making it an ideal place to think deeply, while reflecting on history, life, and art. Even the fabric for the floral drapery and upholstery is the result of a personal quest. Based on an 1830s pattern originally designed for Queen Marie-Amélie, the wife of Louis-Philippe, king of the French between 1830 and 1848, it had disappeared for nearly two centuries until Couturier revived it. "It was a color and weave that hadn't been produced since, and I asked Le Manach if they could re-create it," says Couturier. "To me, that makes this fabric something very special. The library has become the perfect place to read, listen to music, and entertain guests for drinks."

A reclaimed 1820s American entrance portal frames the impressive door to the library. The planter on the right is an eighteenth-century French marble urn.

ABOVE: A nineteenth-century French table purchased from Axel Vervoordt is layered with some of Couturier's favorite decorative finds, including stone obelisks and lighthearted bookends.

OPPOSITE: American columns from the 1820s that were split in half add a sense of grandeur to the room. Louis XVI armchairs by Étienne Avril and window shades feature a Le Manach fabric pattern from the 1820s that Couturier had the company reissue. The reclining chaise is by Emilio Terry.

T

THE
LIVING ROOM

THE EXPANSIVE LIVING ROOM IS THE sun-drenched heart of Couturier's home. "One aspect of French country houses that I've always loved is that the gardens were designed to be best enjoyed from inside the home rather than walking outside," says Couturier. "That's what I tried to achieve in this room." Featuring a seventeen-foot-tall ceiling and enormous windows on all four sides of the room, which provide views out to the lake and onto the garden, the feeling is unmistakably bright, airy, and fresh. "Because it has so many windows and the light is so lovely, it changes throughout the day," says Couturier. "The fabrics and colors shift from morning to afternoon to evening."

To the untrained eye, the more traditional pieces of French furniture may initially give the impression of an eighteenth-century château, but the decoration of the room is infinitely more nuanced than that. Look closely and you'll see covetable examples of early twentieth-century design—a pair of shagreen cocktail tables and a straw marquetry fire screen by Jean-Michel Frank, and a 1950s Maison Jansen sofa that Couturier had duplicated to make a perfect pair—arranged in perfect symmetry. Appearances to the contrary, modern technology isn't banished either. An elaborately carved Alsatian armoire from 1601, with its rare finials still intact, doesn't just provide a visual focal point—it also conceals a television.

In Couturier's opinion, a home's living room shouldn't be a space that's reserved solely for formal entertaining. "I'm happiest in this room," he says. "I just love lying down here with all the dogs while Jeffrey is standing up doing crossword puzzles in the den, because it feels so comfortable and cozy." For amusement, he contemplates the portraits that line the walls. "I have a relationship with the people in those paintings," he says. "I imagine who they were and create whole stories. It's the basis for daydreaming."

At times, he has tried inserting even more contemporary pieces into the room, but Morgan was unimpressed. "I once bought an incredibly beautiful marble armchair, shaped like a bird, by my good friend François-Xavier Lalanne," says Couturier. "I had it sent to Kent, but, when it arrived, Jeffrey called my secretary and said 'Get that loo out of my living room.' So there are certain things I can't do."

OPPOSITE: Wall plaques featuring relief portraits of Roman gods (these two are part of a larger series) hang with seventeenth-century Dutch landscape paintings on the living room wall. The window offers a view over North Spectacle Lake.

OVERLEAF: The seventeen-foot-high room is furnished with an eclectic range of pieces, including Maison Jansen sofas (one original, one reproduction), shagreen cocktail tables and a straw marquetry screen by Jean-Michel Frank, Louis XVI side chairs in Prelle silk, an enormous seventeenth-century Alsatian armoire, and clusters of crystals originally designed by Serge Roche for Elizabeth Arden. A seventeenth-century Gilbert Jackson painting of Lady Elizabeth Dormer, pregnant with the first Duke of Beaufort, hangs above the stately fireplace.

THE LANDING

THERE'S A DEFINITE ADVANTAGE TO ALLOWING A HOUSE
to evolve over time—you can experience how it feels at different times of day, and in different
seasons, and make adjustments. When Couturier first built his house, there was no grand landing like there is today—it was merely a small, enclosed stairway linking the downstairs kitchen
to the upstairs living room. "It was dark," says Couturier, "and it also made the living room dark."

To remedy the situation, he enclosed what was previously a terrace to create a larger in-
door landing between levels and added many new windows. Now the space not only links
the original kitchen and living room but it also functions as a key circulation route, provid-
ing access to the garden and a connection to the dining room. It is also an intimate sitting
area in its own right, and a perfect place to study the landscape while catching one's breath.

Couturier installed some of his most cherished objects here to give it the feel of a gallery. A
nude by George Bellows hangs above the staircase, but most notable of all is a Roman bust of
Faustina the Elder, wife of emperor Antoninus Pius, proudly elevated on a pedestal in the corner. Dating from the third century, it was once part of the Roman Forum. "It's an amazing piece
to have," concedes Couturier. "I just love it."

ABOVE: A third-century Roman bust of Faustina the Elder,
wife of emperor Antoninus Pius, is proudly elevated on a pedestal.

OPPOSITE: A large nude by George Bellows, discovered in the American painter's
studio after his death, hangs over the staircase, along with a work by French artist Édouard Vuillard.

OPPOSITE: Couturier is a passionate collector, and his finds are displayed in
thoughtful arrangements throughout the house. Here, an eighteenth-century Florentine silver horse
shares space with an assortment of sculptural objects and curiosities, including a gilded
figurine of Cleopatra killing herself with a cobra.

ABOVE, TOP: A collection of snuffboxes believed to have been owned by Marie Antoinette.

ABOVE, BOTTOM: Handsome letter openers, including pieces made with ivory and lapis lazuli.

CLOCKWISE, FROM TOP: A seventeenth-century delftware plate, an elephant
figurine from the 1920s, and a bust of Madame du Barry beside an Hermès clock.

OPPOSITE: An eighteenth-century oryx horn is a strong vertical element atop a desk by Joseph Canabas.

C

The
Dining Room

COUTURIER ORIGINALLY BUILT THE HOUSE with a small kitchen and dining area below the living room, but he soon felt the need to expand. "I looked at the way we live and the way we like to entertain, and decided we needed a proper dining room," says Couturier, who drew plans for this new wing in 2005.

The result is one of the most breathtaking spaces on the property, with rows of French doors punctuating both long walls, making the room feel almost like an outdoor pavilion. On one side, the doors can be opened to provide direct access to the garden; on the other, they offer views beyond the meandering driveway. "I wanted something like an orangerie, with the double exposure," says Couturier. "I wanted that wing to be bathed in light." As with all of Couturier's architectural projects, a masterful sense of proportion also elevates the space—in this case, a long, narrow room with slender paneling and soaring ceiling gives the impression of a grand room with a built-in sense of ceremony.

To filter all the sunlight, Couturier turned to the Parisian embroidery atelier Lesage, known for its work on couture gowns for fashion houses such as Chanel, Yves Saint Laurent, and Jean Paul Gaultier, with a design for custom sheer curtains. "I had seen this particular motif, which is a Mughal motif for flowers, and been captivated by it," he says. "It's my little piece of India." The result is among what he considers to be the home's most successful design elements—even if the curtains have had unintended consequences. "Now I don't even take advantage of the view, because I love those curtains so much," he says. "I keep them closed all the time."

OPPOSITE: The dining room represents a mix of times and places. The chandelier is seventeenth-century Dutch, the portrait of the first Earl De La Warr is by English painter Gilbert Jackson, and the truncated crystal columns are twentieth-century pieces by French designer Serge Roche.

LEFT: Upholstered Louis XIV dining chairs provide comfort for lengthy dinnertime conversations. The room is designed to maximize natural light, with two long walls of French doors. An early seventeenth-century Italian mirror hangs above the fireplace. In the corner is a Rouen earthenware urn—France's answer to delftware.

ABOVE: A dining table is set with 1880s Tiffany & Co. silver that originally belonged to Morgan's grandmother, English and French crystal, and plates that were owned by the Duchess of Angoulême, daughter of Louis XVI and Marie Antoinette.

ABOVE: A view from the dining room to the living room landing.
The reproduction eighteenth-century American chairs in the foreground are used
for hosting large dinner parties of more than fourteen people.

OPPOSITE: The linen curtains, a custom design produced by the embroidery
atelier Lesage based on a Mughal motif for flowers, are among Couturier's most prized
possessions and filter sunlight to fill the room with a pleasing glow.

THE KITCHEN

COUTURIER DOESN'T COOK, BUT HE ADORES a beautiful kitchen. Shortly after completing the dining room, he realized that the home's original kitchen no longer suited the evolving character of the house. "The dining room turned things a little more formal," says Couturier, who began sketching plans for a new service kitchen with a direct connection to the rear of the dining room. The change would also free up the first kitchen to be transformed into an informal den.

When designing the new room, the designer pulled from his memories of growing up in grand French houses, where there was a clear distinction between dining and service areas. "When you have an elegant house, you're not ever supposed to smell things cooking," says Couturier. "But as kids we would sit at the kitchen table having our meals, so it was something very happy. I remember coming back from boarding school on Saturdays and the smell I loved most was French fries. My family always had beef roasts on Saturdays. I would arrive late, and our cook would make the most fantastic French fries just for me."

Almost as a counterpoint to the formal dining room, where the table is frequently set with Couturier's vast collections of delicate stemware and china, the kitchen is much more muscular, and nothing within it is overly precious. Robust cabinetry with brass bin pulls is designed to withstand heavy use, professional-grade appliances were selected for function, open shelves keep pots and pans handy, and small appliances are always left on the countertops, ready for use. But even with the inclusion of modern conveniences, the vaulted ceiling and generous natural light make the space feel like something of a cathedral for cooking. However, it is a welcoming space—it is the classic, large-scale country kitchen that promises only to improve with age.

OPPOSITE: The food preparation areas of the grand French houses Couturier grew up in inspired the design of the home's second kitchen. The cabinets, open shelves, marble countertops, and large-scale light fixtures are intended to be simple, robust, and highly functional.

ABOVE: For entertaining, Couturier maintains
an extensive collection of antique glassware, silverware, and ceramics.

OPPOSITE: English and French eighteenth-century glass vessels animate a windowsill.

PRIVATE
QUARTERS

T
HERE IS A CLEAR DIVISION BETWEEN
public and private realms in Couturier's house. The central entrance hall
neatly splits the house into two functional halves. To reach the public areas, including the living room, dining room, and kitchen, you turn toward
the east wing. To reach the private quarters, including the bedrooms, bathrooms, and office, you go west. There is also a definite shift in scale as you
enter the private quarters. Where the living and dining rooms impress with
their open, large-scale spaces, the private rooms are much more intimate.

Couturier's dog Henriette lounges near the fire in a cozy den that was once the
home's primary kitchen. The room is still used for casual meals.

A

THE SITTING ROOM

ALTHOUGH COUTURIER IS A MASTER of mixing different periods and styles, he had a clear historical concept for this ground-floor sitting room. "This little space, for me, is the epitome of a French eighteenth-century room," he says, adding that he set out to make it feel like a protective refuge from inclement weather.

It is also a space that encourages quiet contemplation. Letting your gaze drift to the windows reveals idyllic views of manicured grounds and swaying treetops. Shift your vision to the foreground, and your eyes land upon collections of finely crafted objects and small-scale statuary that Couturier has amassed over the years.

Driving home the designer's desire to make it a typically French room, the space contains a number of particularly impressive antique finds. A pair of armchairs was originally used in Marie Antoinette's bathroom at Fontainebleau. The Louis XVI daybed was made by the famed Parisian furniture maker Georges Jacob. And a small shelving unit was a surprise find, even to Couturier—it had been previously owned by his mother. "It had actually been in our house in Paris," he says. "I had no idea that my mother had sold it, but I found it at a dealer's showroom in New York, and I bought it immediately. Finding something like that is so much fun."

An eighteenth-century neo-Gothic chair and Louis XVI desk by Étienne Avril, which is topped by Nymphenburg porcelain from the 1930s.

LEFT: A daybed by Georges Jacob is lavishly appointed with sumptuous pillows and a fur throw. The eighteenth-century armchair was originally owned by the Duc de Brissac.

ABOVE: The room contains a pair of Louis XVI armchairs from Marie Antoinette's bathroom at the Château de Fontainebleau.

OFFICE

IT DOESN'T GET MUCH MORE SNUG

than Couturier's home office. Although there is plenty of space available on the property, Couturier deliberately made his office the smallest room in the house. Adding to the feeling of complete immersion in a cocooning environment are walls upholstered with Le Manach fabric featuring an 1840s paisley pattern. "I wanted everything to be upholstered for a sense of warmth and coziness," says Couturier. He readily admits that it isn't necessarily the most practical space—the small eighteenth-century French desk, for instance, "is incredibly uncomfortable, but looks good," he says—but it does have the pleasing sense of somewhere private and welcoming, like a secret room that you stumble upon. That feeling is bolstered by a discreet door offering direct access to the garden behind the house, which provides a perfect escape on warm summer days.

ABOVE: A painting of the Grotta Azzurra in Capri, Italy.

OPPOSITE: Walls upholstered in Indian paisley by Le Manach create an enveloping feeling in Couturier's home office. An eighteenth-century Japanese root mirror hangs above a 1920s gilded-bronze table.

I

The Bedroom

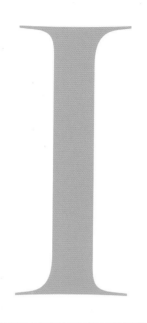

IF THERE IS ONE CONSTANT AT COUTURIER'S house, it is continual experimentation, as he develops new ideas to enhance the rooms he has already created. The bedroom is no exception. When the house was first built, he simply painted the walls white. But he later adjusted them with a compelling detail—C&C Milano linen fabric that runs floor to ceiling and wall to wall. "I thought the paint was a little harsh, so we had it all upholstered in white fabric," says Couturier. "It still looks as if it's painted but the feeling is subtly warmer." The fabric also offers a pleasing touch under the fingertips while dampening sound to create a quiet, restful space.

Come January and February, the textile walls create the feeling of an insulated envelope—a definite advantage for the area. "The first winter we were here was one of those typical New England winters where there was a big snowstorm and then the temperature dropped to -20 degrees Fahrenheit, where it stayed for the months," recalls Couturier. "Everything was encased in ice."

In that kind of environment, the reassuring embrace of fabric, both around the edges of the room and around the bed, creates a room he loves to retreat to. Yet the overall effect is by no means heavy. With light green trim, leggy furniture, and bare wood floors, the room also has a freshness that's ideally suited to spring and summer. Thanks to such thoughtfully layered elements, it is a true four-season room, capable of responding to the area's unpredictable weather.

PRECEDING SPREAD: A portrait of Couturier and Morgan by Gerald Incandela (left). An eighteenth-century banyan, or man's dressing gown, on the landing (right).

LEFT: A mask from New Zealand and a collection of fifth-century B.C. Attic vases sit atop an eighteenth-century American chest of drawers.

OPPOSITE: Custom bed curtains from Chelsea Editions create a sense of warmth and privacy.

Never afraid of contrast, Couturier furnished the
room with a diverse collection of pieces, including an
early American highboy chest and a contemporary
goatskin-covered stool by Hervé Van der Stræten.

LEFT: One of the latest additions to the property is a pair of bathrooms.
The onyx-clad shower is equipped with minimalist fittings, simple benches, and a 1940s set of French shelves.

ABOVE: This space, with soaking tub, is warmed up with wallpaper,
fabric shades, an eighteenth-century Japanese monk's desk, and a Régence armchair.

THE DOGS

FOR COUTURIER, THE FOUR SHIH TZUS THAT ROAM HIS HOUSE—
Bess, Dora, Henriette, and Hercule—are an absolutely essential part of country life. "I've always had
dogs," he says. "They are perfect extensions of yourself." Even though his house is filled with precious
furniture and objects, Couturier's pets are given free rein. "If they dig holes in your furniture, so be
it," he says. "When you live with dogs, you just have to accept that accidents happen, and that's life."

The designer likes nothing more than tuning out the outside world on a beautiful Sunday and play-
ing with his pets all day long, until they finally settle down on their cashmere blankets for a rest. "You
are everything for them," he says. "And you owe it to them to give them the most beautiful lives possible."

OPPOSITE: Dora at rest.

ABOVE, TOP: Despite the upholstered walls, drapery, and fine furniture, Couturier doesn't worry about damage by his beloved pets.

ABOVE, BOTTOM: Dora, Hercule, Bess, and Henriette (left to right).

I

THE GARDENS

"I ABSOLUTELY LOVE MY GARDENS," says Couturier. "They are probably my favorite part of the house." That's a surprising statement for a man who specializes in designing the interiors of buildings—even more so when you consider that the thriving, tightly clipped parterre didn't come easily. When Couturier first built the house, he hired landscape architect Miranda Brooks to implement his vision for a formal garden that recalled the manicured outdoor spaces he had visited during his childhood in France. "She was a genius at designing the layout and structure of the garden," says Couturier. However, he never got to see it grow after it was planted—all of the plants died during an exceptionally harsh first winter that also killed seventy-five of the property's largest hemlocks. The next year, he recruited a different landscape designer who put new plants in the ground—but still they refused to flourish. It was only when he hired a local gardener who had formerly worked for Couturier's next-door neighbor, Oscar de la Renta, that the plants really took root. "The first summer he took care of our garden, everything started blooming," says Couturier. "He just gave it life."

With worries about the longevity of his plantings behind him, Couturier was free to focus on one of his other passions—collecting garden ornaments. "They are a way to punctuate a garden," he says, noting that his garden contains everything from a fourth-century Roman capital to eighteenth-century English urns purchased during his travels. "They carry your eye a certain distance and frame visions, vistas, and views." But, he adds, they should be used selectively for maximum impact. "If left to my own devices, I would have a forest of stone people," he says, noting that Morgan helps keep him from going overboard. "Jeffrey is infinitely more restrained than I am," he notes. "And thank God, because that makes things better."

OPPOSITE: The parterre gardens, created with the assistance of landscape designer Clive Lodge, involve more than two thousand boxwood plants and allées of hornbeam trees.

OVERLEAF: The main house viewed from the bottom of the driveway, with North Spectacle Lake beyond.

OPPOSITE: An ancient Roman capital and pair of early twentieth-century limestone finials create moments of focus and a sense of rhythm.

ABOVE: The doors of the dining pavilion provide direct access to the gardens.

OPPOSITE AND ABOVE: Parterre gardens, punctuated by
garden ornaments and planters, provide year-round sculptural drama.

OPPOSITE AND ABOVE: Gravel pathways and stone steps
run through the manicured gardens behind the main house.

ABOVE: A pair of seventeenth-century Italian
planters from the Palazzo Medici Riccardi in Florence, Italy, at the top of a stone staircase.

RIGHT: A vase from the 1970s is hidden away as a treat to discover during walks.

GUESTHOUSES

W

WHILE COUTURIER IS LARGELY RESPONSIBLE for the main house, with its expanded wings and library pavilion, two other houses on the property reflect Morgan's aesthetic preferences. An architectural historian specializing in early American buildings, Morgan has faithfully nursed these smaller-scale eighteenth-century houses, which are used primarily as guesthouses, back to their original designs and furnished them with pieces that reflect that era's spartan, utilitarian way of living. "Jeffrey tries to stay out of our main house, and I try to say out of the eighteenth-century houses," says Couturier. "What he creates is incredibly beautiful."

The early eighteenth-century Dover House, once slated to be burned, was rescued and moved here from Dover Plains, New York.

THE
DOVER HOUSE

SEEING IT FULLY RESTORED, IT'S HARD to believe that this house was nearly torched by a nearby town's fire department for practice. But when Morgan first saw it, it was in truly dilapidated condition. "It was the oldest remaining house in Dover Plains, New York, and was standing prior to 1710," says Morgan, who had spotted the structure in a farmer's field a few years prior. "When I asked if I could examine the building, he said 'Oh, you're just in time,'" recalls Morgan, because it was scheduled to be burned to the ground.

When Morgan looked inside, he was immediately taken with the structure. "It had beautiful flooring, a great frame, and incredible fireplaces," he says. "It was clear that there were many goodies still there." Knowing he had to act quickly, Morgan made an offer to purchase the house and haul it away. "The farmer seemed surprised that I wanted to buy it," he recalls. "He said 'Take it away, fill in the hole, and it's yours.'" So he did, dismantling the structure board by board, and storing it temporarily in a warehouse.

Morgan and Couturier originally intended to rebuild the structure as the main house on their property, but ran into difficulties with the town, which refused to give them permits because the restored structure wouldn't meet twenty-first-century building codes. When negotiations dragged on, "we put it on hold, kept it in a trailer, and built the other house instead," says Morgan. It wasn't until 2012 that they finally won approval to proceed. But it was worth the wait, says Morgan. "It came out better than we ever could have imagined." Modestly elegant, it stands at the entrance of the property, across from the barn.

An eighteenth-century blanket chest with original paint and blue-and-white woolen blanket, both from Connecticut, at the entrance to the house.

ABOVE: An eighteenth-century lattice-front cupboard from the Hudson Valley
displays a variety of vessels, including a seventeenth-century French pewter charger.

OPPOSITE: An early eighteenth-century William and Mary lowboy from Massachusetts holds a large
Dutch Heemskerk brass candleholder and Friesian carved oak box.

ABOVE: An eighteenth-century Mohawk Valley cupboard contains period delftware chargers and English pewter.

OPPOSITE: A Hudson Valley reeded banister-back armchair by the fireplace, along with early American iron fire tools.

OVERLEAF: An eighteenth-century English oak and iron spice grinder, a seventeenth-century
Spanish lobed vessel, and an eighteenth-century English salt glaze jug (left). A worn Dutch oak table is
surrounded by eighteenth-century American chairs (right).

ABOVE: Despite the presence of modern plumbing,
the bathroom maintains a spartan appearance. The side chair is a Morgan
family relic from the nineteenth century.

RIGHT: A seventeenth-century English oak geometric
carved coffer at the foot of a reproduction bed made up to provide
comforting warmth on cool nights.

ABOVE: The approach to Dover House from the driveway.

RIGHT: A view of the back of the house, which was painstakingly
rebuilt on the site, along with its new gardens.

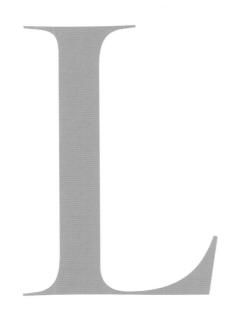

L

THE GATEHOUSE

LOCATED NEAR THE ENTRANCE TO THE property, this is the home that started it all. Morgan bought the eight-hundred-square-foot house, which had been built in 1742, in 1979. "I could see that it was a good early house, even though it was covered up and in ill repair," he says. "There were original things peeping out here and there. The great thing about that house is that all the important stuff got covered over rather than removed." He moved in after a three-year restoration, during which time he peeled away later additions to reveal the original wood structure, clapboard siding, and wide-plank floors, and furnished it with an austere collection of New England antiques.

Couturier first visited in 1997, and wasn't exactly taken with the property upon first glance. "In summer, it had insects everywhere, which drove me crazy; when winter came, it had barely any heat. That was not my sort of thing," says Couturier. "It was amazing to me that Jeffrey could live in the way he did." To provide a little more comfort, the pair soon built a guest cabin modeled on a nearby eighteenth-century schoolhouse. "It had all the conveniences I liked, so we moved our bedroom into the guesthouse," says Couturier. "We'd spend the day in the old house and gardens, and then move across the property to sleep."

Eventually, wanting something larger, they purchased two neighboring lots in 2000, bringing the size of the property up to sixteen acres. "I knew immediately that Jeffrey was emotionally attached to that house to such a degree that I would never be able to make him let it go," says Couturier. So he began dreaming of a new, larger house next door, and drafting plans for the building and property that would realize his vision for a rural paradise.

An eighteenth-century New Hampshire maple desk with original black paint and a Queen Anne side chair of local manufacture offer a place to compose one's thoughts. The hanging shears are the first antique Morgan ever purchased, more than fifty years ago.

ABOVE: A wall cupboard holds delftware plates and eighteenth-century English and American glassware.

OPPOSITE: A collection of eighteenth-century banister-back American chairs at a maple tea table from Rhode Island. The William and Mary highboy is from Massachusetts and the portrait of Abraham Gibson, a Boston merchant, was painted by Ethan Allen Greenwood in 1811.

ABOVE: Morgan at work in the garden.

RIGHT: A view of the grounds. The original house
is on the left; the newer guest cabin is on the right.

D
THE
CITY APARTMENT

DURING THE WEEK, WHEN COUTURIER is in New York, he lives in a twenty-five-hundred-square-foot floor-through apartment located directly above his firm's SoHo office. Although he moved there in 2000, he has utterly transformed the apartment on numerous occasions. "I can try things in this space because I don't live here permanently," he says. "My emotional life isn't here, so I'm less attached to the things that surround me. An apartment is a little bit like a suit—when you get tired of it, you can easily change it to reflect your current taste."

However, the common thread through all those renovations is that Couturier's apartment has served as an urban crash pad that reflects his eclectic interests, including his passion for modern and contemporary design. "This is in direct contrast to what I have in the country in many ways," he says. "Here in the city I have varied, wonderful things from all sorts of different eras." That includes eighteenth-century English paintings and twentieth-century photographs by Couturier's late friend David Seidner; eighteenth-century French rugs and a Deco-era zebra sofa by Jacques Adnet; and ancient curiosities paired with works by contemporary artists and designers such as Missoni Patchwork vases by Stephen Burks. There are also a few family heirlooms, including cabinets by Alfred Porteneuve that were originally designed for his grandfather's office.

In its current incarnation, the apartment presents Couturier's take on open-concept living. Infinitely softer and more comfortable than an austere loft, it nevertheless blends different living functions. The sleeping area, work space, and bathroom are separated by a pair of low curved walls and are allowed to spill into the main sitting room. "The way I live here is different than the way I live in the country," says Couturier. "It all works together as one big room."

In the library, an Ernest Boiceau rug anchors a Louis XVI table, which is surrounded by a set of 1790s chairs from Copenhagen. Glass shelves and an early twentieth-century cabinet by André Sornay create space for storage. The framed photograph of a Cuban interior is by Michæl Eastman; and the portrait above the cabinet is by David Seidner.

ABOVE: A work by Gerald Incandela above the 1920s mahogany cabinet by Alfred Porteneuve, which was originally designed for Couturier's grandfather.

OPPOSITE: A portrait of Couturier by Gerald Incandela hangs in the living room. On the floor, a mid-nineteenth-century Persian rug is layered on top of a white rug.

ABOVE: Couturier in his living room. The early twentieth-century oak and porcelain table is by
Jacques Adnet and Maurice Savin, and the sconces are by Armand-Albert Rateau. The contemporary
Missoni Patchwork vases are by Stephen Burks.

OPPOSITE: A 1940s French table lamp is paired with a mirror and table by Charles Rennie Mackintosh.
The reflected painting is by Sébastien de Ganay.

Couturier's living room is a study in symmetry, where furniture and objects from different eras effortlessly mix together.

LEFT: A photograph by Ron Agam hangs above a Couturier-designed suede sofa and a 1930s Frances Elkins cocktail table. The plaster screen is by Marc Bankowsky.

OVERLEAF: In the office, a pair of ebony and tortoiseshell mirrors sets off an eighteenth-century portrait by Richard Cosway. A Jacques Adnet sofa upholstered in faux zebra and a pair of 1930s French armchairs offer deep comfort. The rug is eighteenth-century French.

ABOVE: A photograph by Robert Mapplethorpe
above a 1940s French bed.

RIGHT: A pair of Louis XV bergères flank
Couturier's desk, which is topped by red leather desk accessories
by Jacques Adnet for Hermès. The photographic portraits
are by David Seidner.

PART
II

SELECT PROJECTS

WHEN DESIGNING FOR OTHERS, COUTURIER aims to create residences that are genuine representations of each client's personality and spirit. That results in dramatically different homes that encompass a broad range of styles, from traditional eighteenth-century French houses to palatial vacation villas to ultra-contemporary apartments. "My projects are direct reflections of the people," he says. "The work is so varied that it's almost impossible for my clients to think they're going to get any one thing." Rather than a singular designer signature, they will emerge from the design, construction, and decorating process with a home that represents the ultimate in personalization.

It's not surprising that many of Couturier's clients are repeat customers who ask him to create numerous residences for them around the globe. Although their homes may look radically different from Couturier's country estate in Kent or his SoHo apartment, no project is any less personal. "I remain incredibly close with almost all of my clients," he says. "They become very close friends."

PRECEDING SPREAD: A view of an English country house by architect Edwin Lutyens with interiors redesigned by Couturier.

ABOVE: A colorful nook in a New York home.

RIGHT: An apartment on Manhattan's Fifth Avenue.

W

CUIXMALA

WHEN COUTURIER WAS ONLY THIRTY-three, just one year after establishing his own firm, he landed a job of unimaginable proportions—the complete design of Cuixmala, financier Sir James Goldsmith's twenty-thousand-acre Mexican vacation estate, from the monumental architecture to the smallest of decorative details. Goldsmith had already hired one team of architects and builders in Mexico, but was disappointed by their proposals. "Jimmy had told them he wanted palaces," says Couturier. "But for a normal person, a palace is difficult to translate into reality—it's a fairy tale." For a designer who had spent his childhood touring France's most fabulous residences, however, it was almost second nature.

Goldsmith gave Couturier four weeks to generate a concept, during which time the designer drew day and night, generating lavish color renderings by hand. When Couturier presented them, Goldsmith immediately retained him as his exclusive architect and designer. "We had two years and a thousand workers to build it all," says Couturier, noting that it was a colossal task. "It was like building a whole town." The job included guesthouses scattered across the area's hilltops; a village for pilots, secretaries, nannies, and other staff; a separate village for workers; and two notable palatial homes—La Loma, Goldsmith's sixty-thousand-square-foot mountaintop residence, which was topped by a cupola tiled with a bold blue-and-yellow herringbone pattern; and a separate seaside residence for his ex-wife, which was formed by interlocking circular rooms. "It was an incredible, all-consuming experience," says Couturier, who would go on to design other residences for Goldsmith, along with a private jet. "Jimmy was incredibly influential to me, and became much more than just a client."

The herringbone tiled cupola of La Loma, the main house at Cuixmala in Mexico.

ABOVE: The grand entrance to the sixty-thousand-square-foot residence.

OPPOSITE: One of the property's many water features, in a courtyard that blurs the boundary between inside and out.

LEFT: Sunlight filters through custom sandstone panels made in Jaipur and wooden Mughal *jalis*.

ABOVE: Colorful textiles purchased in Jaipur, India, create an inviting, summery feeling throughout the home.

RIGHT: A hillside staircase descends to a pool and beach below the seaside house.

OVERLEAF: The estate's private stables. Comprising twenty thousand acres, the grounds provide plenty of opportunities for exploring on horseback (left). Planters containing small-scale flowers and large-scale palm trees add to the property's lush, paradisiacal feeling (right).

ABOVE: A poolside *palapa*.

RIGHT: The seaside residence, composed of interlocking circular volumes, is nestled in the hillside above a sprawling pool.

A

Volcano House

AMONG THE MANY RESIDENCES COUTURIER
designed for Sir James Goldsmith was a sprawling hacienda and former coffee plantation at the foot of Mexico's Colima volcano. Dating from the 1860s, the original manor house had fallen into disrepair
by the middle of the twentieth century, and had been the subject of a
smaller renovation in 1978. Asked to reimagine the property, Couturier's
approach wasn't just to restore the home to its former glory, but to expand it considerably, including a whole new second courtyard that
mirrors the original one, new living and dining rooms, and multiple
bedrooms. Throughout the house, fifteen-foot-high vaulted brick ceilings, weathered wooden doors, fireplaces made from black volcanic
rock, and locally produced terra-cotta tiles create an immediate sense
of history. Beyond the architecture, he drew plans for the surrounding landscape, including terraced gardens and elaborate water features.

Once it was built, Goldsmith asked his daughter, Alix Marcaccini,
to lead the decoration. She began filling the rooms with the finest,
large-scale antiques she could find in Mexico and abroad—carved
wood armchairs and chandeliers, enormous mirrors with ornate
frames, and wrought-iron beds and candelabras. Considering that the
sprawling home has twenty-seven bedrooms, which were typically
filled with guests whenever Goldsmith visited, it was no easy feat.

Finally completed in 1995, the estate is an archetypal Mexican hacienda,
designed to take maximum advantage of the site's breathtaking natural
features. "That's what it was long ago, and what it is once again," says
Couturier. Indeed, the revived home was completed with such authentic
details that local authorities gave it landmark status almost as soon as it
was finished. "The State of Colima came and declared it a historic place
and forbade us to change anything," says Couturier. "To me, that's a definite
sign that we got it right."

A view from the house to the nearby Colima volcano in Mexico.

OPPOSITE: The exterior of the house.

ABOVE: Couturier rebuilt an original courtyard and then added a second, both with convincing architectural details.

Couturier re-created the architecture of the house, which overlooks a former coffee plantation, so as to have it appear absolutely authentic, including vaulted brick ceilings. Sir James Goldsmith's daughter, Alix Marcaccini, led the decoration.

RIGHT: The dining room is rich with robust carved wood furniture and chandeliers and large-scale silver accessories.

OVERLEAF: An elevated terrace is an ideal location for taking in the area's rugged beauty (left). Wrought-iron outdoor furniture paired with thick, generous cushions encourages easy indoor-outdoor living (right).

Couturier designed not only the architecture of the house, but also the surrounding gardens, a vital component of the hacienda's charm that couldn't be left to chance.

#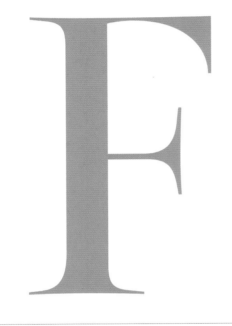

PARIS HÔTEL PARTICULIER

FOR COUTURIER, EVERY INTERIOR DESIGN project is personal, but some are exceptionally so. In this case, one of his oldest and closest friends hired him to design an apartment occupying the top two floors of a Parisian *hôtel particulier*. For Couturier, it was a homecoming of sorts—he had actually met his client in the very same house when they were only teenagers, long before he founded his interior design firm.

When the new owner took control, she insisted that the interior be made to look much more contemporary, in contrast to the exterior. "We wanted her apartment to be spare and considered, because that's who she is," says Couturier. "It's a French apartment without all the French flourishes—the decorations and ornaments and all that."

There are still fine examples of eighteenth-century French and English furniture, but they are used in limited numbers and counterbalance more surprising elements, such as a pair of clean-lined sofas upholstered in fiery stripes and boldly graphic contemporary art. These pieces pop against a crisp, white architectural envelope that offers a streamlined take on decorative woodwork without concealing the building's original identity. Overall, it's a timeless, curated look that isn't limited to any one era. "It's her individual voice," says Couturier, "not what people expect for that kind of home."

Chippendale armchairs and eighteenth-century Japanese Imari vases become strong sculptural statements in this traditional French apartment.

ABOVE: A graphic black-and-white painting by Pierre Soulages, photograph by Andreas Serrano, and boldly striped sofas punctuate a crisp, architectural envelope, giving the apartment an immediate, contemporary appeal.

OPPOSITE: Pared-down classic architectural details reinforce the apartment's fresh and airy feel while making the furniture, accessories, and artwork the center of attention.

W

UPPER EAST SIDE APARTMENT

WORKING WITH A YOUNG FAMILY ON New York's Upper East Side, it would have been easy for Couturier to build upon a two-level home's good architectural bones, and deliver a respectable, traditional apartment with impressively luxurious finishes. But he is never one to take the expected route. Well aware that his clients were cultured, worldly travelers with a deep appreciation for contemporary art and cutting-edge style, Couturier knew that something staid simply wouldn't do.

Instead, he created a relaxed, curated home that's all about personal style. "I wanted to make the house comfortable and easy, formal and informal, French and American, and a reflection of their diverse interests and similarities," says Couturier. "The owners are both incredibly decisive and sure of their tastes and opinions." Peppered with an international mix of furniture, art, and accessories, the completed home has statement-making pieces around every corner. In the living room, for instance, eighteenth-century French chairs are a striking contrast to a pair of Milo Baughman armchairs with chrome backs and a cluster of contemporary faceted tables by Mattia Bonetti. In the library, traditional dark wood paneling sets off a shapely 1960s Boomerang desk by Maurice Calka and tufted leather lounge chair by Walter and Moretti.

But in addition to finds from spectacular shopping expeditions in Europe and the United States, the apartment provides space for family heirlooms to shine. Most striking of all is a collection of eighteenth- and nineteenth-century Persian rugs that one of the client's parents originally purchased in Iran. Underpinning many of the rooms, they are a constant reminder that this apartment is not merely a trophy home—it is a tailored expression of one family's history, interests, and aspirations.

A 1950s American sunburst mirror hangs above a black amphora vase, atop an ebony Regency cabinet with mother-of-pearl inlay.

OPPOSITE: The cocktail table is formed by a cluster of faceted modules by Mattia Bonetti. The painting is by Jean Dubuffet.

ABOVE: The living room contains a broad mix of furniture, from eighteenth-century French chairs to chrome-backed twentieth-century armchairs by Milo Baughman.

OVERLEAF: In the dining room, a dramatic chandelier by Hervé Van der Stræten hangs above a 1980s Italian table, which is surrounded by Maison Jansen chairs upholstered in suede. The photograph is by Candida Höfer (left). A lounge chair and ottoman by Walter & Moretti and a Boomerang desk by Maurice Calka in the library (right).

ABOVE: The master bedroom's custom Couturier-designed bed features hand-embroidered details by Marquise de Laborde. The articulating sconces are by Urban Archæology.

OPPOSITE: A vintage 1960s French armchair and chest of drawers by Martin Szekely. The artwork on the mantel is by Ian Davenport.

W

FIFTH AVENUE APARTMENT

WHEN THE OWNER OF THIS MANHATTAN apartment told Couturier she desired the interior architecture of her eight-thousand-square-foot home to look typically French, the designer wanted her to be absolutely sure. So he scheduled a fact-finding trip for the woman, her financier husband, and himself to the heart of Paris. "For two days, we didn't buy anything," he says. "We just visited the Musée Nissim de Camondo, top museums, private houses, and artisan ateliers," such as Féau & Cie, the revered maker of reproduction decorative woodwork. Following that whirlwind education in French design, the client confirmed her desires, and Couturier got to work.

However, Couturier's client also had specific ideas about the furniture. While she coveted traditional architectural details, she wanted her home to have statement-making contemporary sofas, chairs, tables, and lamps. "She wanted something more extravagant and crazier" than exclusively French eighteenth-century furniture, says Couturier. At the same time, she had suggestions for the color palette. "From the beginning, she wanted an Hermès orange room," recalls Couturier. "And she wanted a pink living room."

Combining such disparate elements into a cohesive whole is a perfectly natural assignment for Couturier, who sourced Louis XVI armchairs, Deco-era masterworks by designers such as Eugène Printz and Jacques Adnet, and sculptural tables and light fixtures by contemporary designers like Hervé Van der Straeten, Ron Arad, and Claude and François-Xavier Lalanne. Set off by electric hits of color throughout the home, including a signature orange-and-brown-paneled study, the result is anything but tame. "There's a decoupling between the furniture and the walls, and a real tension between those two things," says Couturier. "She wanted to do something that would have an impact in the social circles they play in." Consider it mission accomplished—this design never fails to elicit visceral reactions.

Paneling and moldings by Féau & Cie and Versailles parquet give the apartment an immediate sense of history, bolstered by a pair of Louis XVI bergères.

OPPOSITE: A contemporary bronze and crystal chandelier by Hervé Van der Stræten hints that this is anything but a typical eighteenth-century French apartment. The curtains are custom embroidered silk.

ABOVE: A pair of Vosges sconces flanks a Croco console by Claude Lalanne in the entry hall.

Two curvaceous polished stainless-steel tables by Ron Arad in the dining room are surrounded by Karl Springer dining chairs upholstered in lavender velvet and green silk. The ceiling fixture is by Eugène Printz.

ABOVE: The living room has multiple seating areas that can be reconfigured on a whim. Here, a Ueli Berger sofa and zebra rug anchor one corner of the space.

OPPOSITE: A Louis XV *canapé à confident*, Louis XVI bergères, and a stool by Michel Boyer are clustered around a cocktail table by Mattia Bonetti. The rug is by Diurne.

Paneling painted a bright Hermès orange and brown enliven the family room, along with a Serpentine sofa by Vladimir Kagan and coffee table by Mattia Bonetti.

ABOVE: A 1930s sofa by Leleu is the perfect fit for a nook in a woman's office.

OPPOSITE: A cowhide rug stitched in a floral pattern from the Rug Company,
silk curtains with tassel tiebacks, and soft pink and gray paneling by Féau & Cie create an
unmistakably feminine environment.

A

Midtown
Manhattan
Apartment

ALTHOUGH MANY OF COUTURIER'S PROJECTS mix different periods and styles, the wife of a prominent Polish businessman asked the designer to push the needle to the ultra-contemporary end of the design spectrum for her forty-five-hundred-square-foot Midtown Manhattan pied-à-terre. Her direction was clear—create a sophisticated home that is as unapologetically fresh and forward looking as possible. Couturier relished the challenge of steering clear of centuries-old antiques, noting that "there is nothing more boring than repeating oneself over and over again."

Organized like a gallery, with white walls and light wood floors, the completed apartment presents furniture with striking sculptural forms created by some of today's most cutting-edge designers, including Joris Laarman, Nendo, and Aranda/Lasch. To assemble the collection, Couturier, who regularly attends international design fairs to identify and track emerging talents, arranged appointments with some of his favorite galleries and then led his client on a breathtaking, worldly shopping spree, lasting two days in New York and two days in Paris. By the time they stopped, they had acquired almost all of the major furniture pieces the apartment would require.

However, Couturier also knows that gallerylike homes can feel impersonal, and that a comfortable residence requires more intimate spaces. To add depth and dimension to the apartment, he gave each of the five bedrooms a different personality, from warm and inviting to playfully bright and colorful. The master bedroom is the coziest of the bunch, despite its generous size, a feeling he created with luxuriously textured carpet, pleated velvet wall covering, and custom bronze-colored wall panels made from liquid metals and resins that offer a Deco-inspired representation of the Manhattan skyline. "You often feel that these very striking modern apartments are like pieces of art themselves, not places you want to live in," says Couturier. But by creating layers of texture, and a series of rooms that gradually reveal themselves, this modern home invites you to slow down and settle in.

Bleached oak floors set off statement-making pieces,
including a polished stainless-steel candelabrum by Joost van Bleiswijk, felted wool
sheep by Ronél Jordaan, and a mirror by Hervé Van der Stræten.

OPPOSITE: In the living room, a pair of Zeta chairs by Paul Tuttle, a Crochet chair by Marcel Wanders, a marble side table by Joris Laarman, and lamps by Hervé Van der Stræten join a Couturier-designed custom sofa with a Corian base. The room partition is by Peter Lane.

ABOVE: The dining room is furnished with limited-edition contemporary design, including a resin and metal dining table by Joris Laarman, a floor lamp by Mattia Bonetti, a sideboard by Aranda/Lasch, and a wing chair and footstool by Kranen/Gille.

OPPOSITE: The study is furnished with a custom daybed upholstered in Velours Klee by Clarence House, a trestle desk by Alessandro Albrizzi, and bronze chair by Pedro Useche. The curtains are laser-cut microsuede.

ABOVE: Walls upholstered in pleated velvet and a custom Couturier-designed bed in silk velvet create a soft, soothing environment in the master bedroom. Custom closet doors depicting the New York skyline in liquid metals and resins are by Based Upon.

I
NY Downtown Apartments

IN A BURGEONING NEIGHBORHOOD FOR NEW York's creative designers, retailers, and restaurateurs, a couple asked Couturier to design a pair of apartments that are located in the same building, but on separate floors. The arrangement allows their international family to accommodate relatives and friends when they visit the city, without necessarily putting everyone together.

To create a sense of continuity between the apartments, Couturier applied a common design concept—install an exciting mix of contemporary and vintage modern furniture that is in keeping with the structure's avant-garde exterior (which was designed by architects Herzog & de Meuron) and enliven the spaces with potent bursts of solid color and show-stopping art. "The challenge was to give personality to these white boxes, and we did it with color," says Couturier. "We used more color in those apartments—long surfaces of it—than we ever had before."

That includes niches painted a bright, juicy orange and feature walls in bedrooms finished with aqua Venetian plaster. Vibrant hits of green, blue, and pink are delivered via furniture, accessories, and art. One apartment is a twenty-four-hundred-square-foot three-bedroom unit; the other is a comparatively small eleven-hundred-square-foot one-bedroom. However, neither space was considered more important than the other. They are essentially two wings of the same private residence, which just happen to be separated by a public hallway and elevator.

OPPOSITE: In the dining area of one apartment, a vintage Poul Henningsen Artichoke lamp is suspended from a lacquered ceiling before an orange Venetian plaster wall. The dining set is by Verner Panton, and the photograph is by Michæl Eastman.

OVERLEAF: In the living room, a series of twelve prints by Rachel Whiteread hangs above a Cassina sectional sofa by Piero Lissoni. The vintage marble and bronze coffee table is by Angelo Mangiarotti.

ABOVE: A series of works by Eduardo Paolozzi on the wall of the master bedroom. The earthenware vases are mid century American pieces by Clyde Burt (large) and Harrison McIntosh.

OPPOSITE: A wall hanging made from woven coat hangers by Federico Uribe is installed on a Venetian plaster wall. The walnut chair, from 1973, is by Archotypo Studio.

ABOVE: In the other apartment, the dining area is filled with curvaceous forms, including a wavy multicolored rug by Paul Smith for the Rug Company and dining chairs by Ron Arad for Moroso.

OPPOSITE: A discreet bar unit by Pierre Paulin in the living room. The painting on the wall is by Sol LeWitt.

OVERLEAF: Ron Arad's twisting Victoria & Albert sofa adds a playful note to the living room. The white leather armchairs are 1960s Italian and the coffee table is by Maison Jansen.

In the master bedroom, a custom Couturier-designed bed is covered in handwoven cashmere by Chapas Textiles. The photo of Ludwig Mies van der Rohe's Farnsworth House is by Hiroshi Sugimoto.

I

ENGLISH COUNTRY HOUSE

IT'S DIFFICULT TO IMAGINE A MORE challenging, yet deeply rewarding design commission than this—renovate and restore a sprawling country estate of epic proportions that is among the storied British architect Sir Edwin Lutyens's greatest masterpieces. The property is so large that neither Couturier nor the owners are able to say precisely how big it is.

What they did know was this: the English country house, built from white chalk in 1904, is one of Lutyens's best-known, most captivating works, and although it was used as a boarding school for decades, its interior detailing was still largely intact. "The boarding school administration had walled in all the precious woodwork and plasterwork," says Couturier. "Everything was protected, which is very rare." In the beginning, he considered doing what most people would do with such a historic home—a straightforward, faithful restoration. "The temptation is to go through historical images of surviving Lutyens houses, which were all furnished with Queen Anne sixteenth- and seventeenth-century furniture," he says. "But the owners wanted the opposite of that." So although they retained all of the original architectural details, says Couturier, "we decided to furnish it with this very contemporary streak of furniture, objects, and art that give the whole house a certain dynamic tension."

Doing so required shopping on an epic scale. Once a month, Couturier and his assistants combed London stores and showrooms, looking for pieces that they believed would be ideal additions to the home. They shipped forty to fifty items to the property at a time, installed them, and presented their selections to the clients. Some pieces made the cut—the rest were returned to the dealers. "It was waves of furniture, depositing a few things each time," says Couturier, noting that they followed the process for two years before the whole house was finally furnished with a suitably edgy mix of new and old.

In a home that could have easily been made to look dusty, the result is incredibly uplifting, and an unmistakable reflection of the owners' personalities. "People who slip into these historical houses have a tendency to forget themselves, and to become the house," says Couturier. "But they didn't fall for that trap. In this case, the house became them. I think that's very important."

The driveway to the house, designed by architect Edwin Lutyens in 1904.

ABOVE: A stainless-steel Well-Tempered chair by Ron Arad in the vestibule.

OPPOSITE: The oak staircase and plasterwork is original, as designed by Lutyens. The suspended lamp is a reproduction of one of the architect's Mercury Ball light fixtures.

OVERLEAF: A sinuous Golden Ribbon light fixture by Ingo Maurer ripples through the paneled library. The marble columns and plasterwork are original (left). An alcove in the library is illuminated with a pair of 1950s floor lamps by Boris Lacroix. The custom sofa is upholstered in handwoven silk and yak wool from Chapas Textiles. The ottoman is upholstered in a nineteenth-century paisley shawl (right).

The 1940s wing chair, upholstered in original
Nigerian goat leather, is by Frits Henningsen. The pair
of armchairs at the fireplace is by Vladimir Kagan.
On the ottoman is a sculpture by Diego Giacometti,
completed in 1977.

ABOVE: The drawing room is furnished with a polished stainless-steel coffee table by Mattia Bonetti, Danish armchairs by Eva and Nils Koppel, and a pair of custom sofas.

OPPOSITE: A glass-topped table by Maurizio Cattelan and chairs by Victor Courtray create a playful area for games. The floor lamp is 1960s French, and the console is by Ico Parisi.

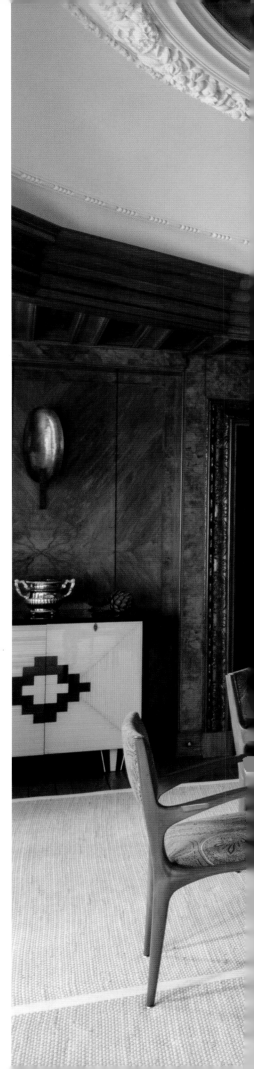

ABOVE, TOP: A convex mirror by Barnaby Barford.

ABOVE, BOTTOM: A bronze bench by François-Xavier Lalanne before the dining room fireplace.

RIGHT: The dining room's original burled walnut paneling and plasterwork
is enlivened with a brass and glass Arredoluce chandelier by Gio Ponti, dining chairs by
Carlo De Carli, and an oak marquetry and bronze table by Hervé Van der Stræten.

Original Lutyens details in the billiard room include the billiard table, which is carved from solid chalk. The billiard light is a bronze reproduction of the original lost oak fixture.

Brave new additions to the billiard room
include a free-form leather sofa by Zaha
Hadid for Sawaya & Moroni and a birch log
coffee table by Fredrikson Stallard.
The earthenware stool and pots under the
arches are by Claude Conover.

LEFT: In the dining room, a pendant lamp by Max Ingrand for Fontana Arte hangs above a Florence Knoll table with marble top and Knoll Tulip chairs by Eero Saarinen. The oak paneling is by Couturier.

OVERLEAF: Reproduction Lutyens chandeliers hang in the ballroom. New additions include wall lamps by Tom Dixon, baseball-glove-shaped Jœ chairs by Gionatan de Pas, and linen curtains embroidered by Jean-François Lesage.

OPPOSITE: A bench by Brodie Neill and vintage Moroccan carpets soften the corridor.

ABOVE: Porcelain vessels by Felicity Aylieff are displayed on a windowsill.

ABOVE: A lounge chair by Pierre Paulin and a wrought iron and
travertine coffee table by Jean Royère in a bay of the master bedroom.

RIGHT: A parchment-covered coffee table by André Arbus
sits at the foot of a custom Couturier-designed bed with draped linen panels
in the master bedroom. The bedside tables are by Claude Lalanne.

A gilded egg-shaped chest by Garouste & Bonetti and artwork by
Yoshitomo Nara create a frankly contemporary statement in the
master dressing room. The upholstered oak stools are 1930s French,
and the floor lamp is by Felix Agostini.

A guest bedroom is furnished with a custom
Couturier-designed sofa upholstered in cowhide and
a pair of 1970s Brazilian chrome and wood tables.
The armchair is by Jacques Quinet.

ABOVE: A pair of 1960s faux bamboo campaign-style *étagères* flanks a fireplace
in a spacious guest bathroom with freestanding claw-foot tub.

OPPOSITE: A 1940s FontanaArte mirror and a fish-shaped Santa Cruz
Islands platter are displayed above a fireplace in a guest bedroom. The glass and bronze
pendant lamp is a Lutyens reproduction, the leather club chairs are 1920s French,
and the curtains are made from Christopher Hyland fabric.

OVERLEAF: A 1960s teak desk by Nanna Ditzel and a 1950s oak and rattan chair
by Louis Sognot are positioned to take advantage of the expansive views. The curtain fabric
is by Robert Kime, and the bed is by Josef Frank.

POSTFACE

HAVING THE GOOD FORTUNE TO count Robert Couturier among my dearest friends (if not to have engaged his peerless professional services), I once gleaned from him a bit of design wisdom that neatly encapsulates, I think, his underlying aesthetic philosophy. In Biarritz a few summers ago for a weekend party at another friend's (magnificent, Couturier-designed) house, Robert and I went into town with our hostess to poke about in a respected *antiquaire*'s shop. Each of us unearthed a treasure: our hostess found a set of charming antique dishes, painted with scenes of Biarritz in another age; Robert, a massive yet astonishingly delicate sterling-silver wine pourer shaped like a fully rigged galleon; and I, a bolt of neoclassically patterned toile de Jouy from the 1790s. Elated at my find, and emboldened by Robert's assurance that the toile would indeed suit the guest room in my tiny cottage back in Connecticut, I proceeded to dash around the shop asking for his opinion on a hodgepodge of other things that had caught my eye: a weather-beaten mermaid from a ship's prow, a framed suite of grand tour intaglios, a Victorian dinner gong, a sunburst mirror small enough, I had been pleased to notice, to fit into my carry-on luggage for the flight home. Courteous as always, Robert gamely accompanied me from one pointless object to the next, proffering a few mild, noncommittal remarks about each one. But when we got to the sunburst mirror, which upon nearer inspection displayed a woeful lack of craftsmanship in its carving and gilding, he could no longer contain himself. "*Mais chérie, ce n'est pas* fin" ("But darling, it isn't *fine*"), he exclaimed—using "fine" not in the American sense of "all right," but in the profound, and profoundly French, sense of "elegant," "rarefied," "re-*fine*d." No sooner had he said the words than I saw that Robert was right: the mirror wasn't fine. There was nothing special or inspiring about it, nothing to justify its inclusion in an environment that, if one cares at all about beauty, ought to be as visually agreeable and soothing as possible: one's house. And I realized that not only had he just given me the litmus test by which I might evaluate any of my own future interior-decor decision for myself—he had also expressed with characteristic astuteness the principle that unifies all of his projects, no matter how stylistically diverse. Robert describes his privileged childhood in Paris as "disconnected from reality," but it is precisely the triumph of artfulness over reality, of harmonious refinement over the unconsidered chaos of a harried and careless world, that comprises his signature and defines his achievement. Steeped since birth in the most sophisticated, exactingly conceived, and rigorously upheld principles of elegance ever devised by a culture in the West—the infinitely subtle codes of taste, etiquette, and *arts de vivre* perfected and preserved by France's old-line leisure classes—Robert never does, says, acquires, or creates anything that isn't *fine*. To spend time in one of his houses, or in his company, is thus to be transported into a world of consummate "*luxe, calme et volupté*" (luxury, tranquility, sensuous delight), to use a phrase from Charles Baudelaire, one of the many great French writers Robert, in his fineness, knows by heart. If such a world is disconnected from reality, then it is in the best way imaginable—as a little foretaste of paradise.

—Caroline Weber

A sculpture by Jean René Gauguin, son of Paul Gauguin, sits atop an 1820s French ebony cabinet with copper inlay.

ACKNOWLEDGMENTS

I WOULD LIKE TO ACKNOWLEDGE AND THANK EVERY person who made *Designing Paradises* a reality.

First, to Sandy Gilbert, my Rizzoli editor, and Katharina Plath-Nourry, my attentive PR lady, who are the true reason why this book came to be. Without your persistence and patience with me (it is not always easy to pin me down and you did it so effortlessly and always with kindness), along with your intelligence, sensitivity, and skill, this book would still be a project. Also, to Tim Street-Porter, for his light-filled and elegant photography; to Tim McKeough, for his clarity of thought; and Edward Leida, for his beautiful book design.

On equal footing, to my husband, Jeffrey Morgan, who is the other half of our paradise and a true artist, who re-created the two intimate "monuments" (houses on our Kent property) in your pure New England taste.

To Nora Sherry, Joey Ramirez, and David Renner, whose attention to details makes our lives in Kent so wonderfully enjoyble. And, of course, to our dogs, Henriette, Bess, Hercule, and Dora, who are the souls of our houses—it would probably be true to say that these are their houses.

To some of my closest friends: Sir James Goldsmith, Laure Boulay de La Meurthe, John and Barbara Vogelstein, Beatrice Stern and Cecile David-Weill, Andrew Solomon and John Habich, David Solomon and Sarah Long Solomon, Anne Hearst and Jay McInerney, Amy Fine Collins, Ania Starak, and Fred Iseman, among others. Thank you for believing in me when I did not believe in myself—I owe the career I have today to you.

To Celine Grillat, whose intelligent guidance and love help me to see clear skies instead of clouds each and every day.

To all the wonderful people who work in my office: Sally Ann Calabrese, Aamir Khandwala, Michael Young, Abram Muljana, Jared Austin, Brian O'Connor, Robert Rossi, Rosa Torabi, and Roque Rey. Your intelligence, taste, and extreme attention are what give flesh to my dreams.

To the love of my dear friends Carolyne Roehm and Caroline Weber, who wrote incredibly kind words about my work and me in *Designing Paradises*.

Last but not least, to Isaac Mizrahi, my long-lost brother. Without your humor, life would be a lot less pleasurable.

To life with all its wonders and all its horrors—without one, the other cannot exist.

—Robert Couturier

Photography Credits

Bill Abranowicz: Pages 149, 150, 151, 152, 153, 154, 155, 157, 159, 160–161, and 163

Zach DeSart: Pages 14 (bottom right), 106, 107, 119, 158, 162, 164–165, 166, and 167

Farhad Farman-Farmaian: author photograph on jacket flap

Gianni Franchellucci: Pages 14 (top right, top left), 169, 170, 171, 172, 173, 175, 176–177, 178, 179, 180, 182– 183, and 184–185

John M. Hall: Pages 8, 78, and 79

Peter Margonelli: Pages 14 (bottom center) and 181

Keith Scott Morton: Page 118

Tim Street-Porter: Pages 2, 5, 6, 10, 13, 14 (top, center, and bottom left), 16–17, 19, 20–21, 22, 24–25, 26, 27, 29, 30, 31, 33, 34–35, 36, 37, 38, 39, 40, 41, 42, 43, 44, 45, 46, 47, 48, 49, 50, 51, 52–53, 55, 56, 57, 58, 59, 60, 61, 62, 63, 64–65, 66, 67, 68, 69, 71, 72–73, 74, 75, 76, 77, 78, 79, 80, 81, 82, 83, 84, 85, 86, 87, 88, 89, 90, 91, 92, 93, 94, 95, 96, 97, 98, 99, 100, 101, 102, 103, 104, 105, 108–109, 110–111, 112–113, 114, 115, 116–117, 121, 122, 123, 124, 125, 126–127, 128, 129, 130, 131, 133, 134, 135, 136–137, 138–139, 140, 141–142, 143, 187, 188, 189, 190, 191, 192–193, 194, 195, 196, 197, 198–199, 200–201, 202–203, 204–205, 206, 207, 208, 209, 210–211, 212–213, 214, 215, 216–217, 218–219, 220, 222, and front and back jacket

Laurence Vetu-Gallud: Pages 145, 146, and 147

Caption, Page 2
Busts of Marie Antoinette and Louis XVI are paired with an eighteenth-century
English vessel proclaiming "A death to all Jacobins."

Casewrap: A detail of Robert Couturier's Kent dining room linen curtains—a custom design produced
by the embroidery atelier Jean-François Lesage for Couturier—is reproduced on the front and back covers.

First published in the United States of America in 2014
by Rizzoli International Publications, Inc.
300 Park Avenue South
New York, NY 10010
www.rizzoliusa.com

2014 2015 2016 2017 / 10 9 8 7 6 5 4 3 2 1

Printed in China

ISBN 13: 978-0-8478-4368-8
Library of Congress Control Number: 2014942045

Project Editor: Sandra Gilbert
Art direction by Edward Leida of Edward Leida Design with assistance from Athena Manolopoulos